W9-BXN-563

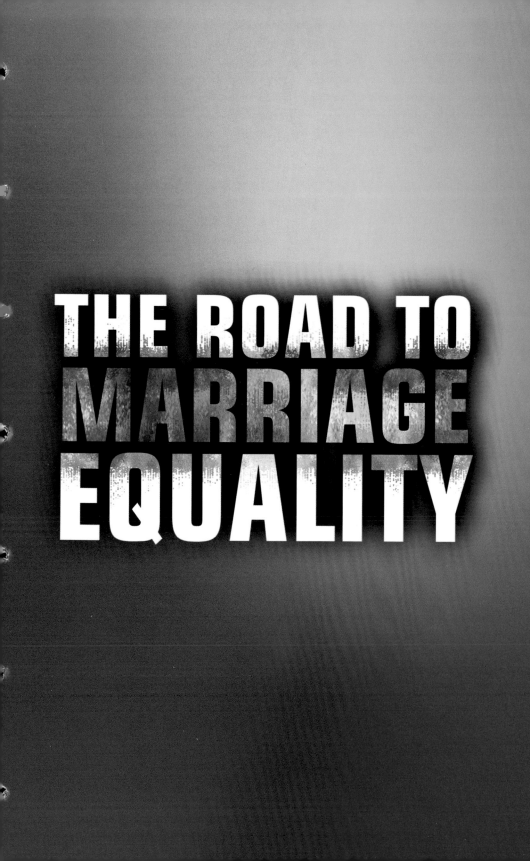

THE ROAD TO MARRIAGE EQUALITY

THE HISTORY OF THE LGBTQ+ RIGHTS MOVEMENT™

THE ROAD TO MARRIAGE EQUALITY

JOHN MAZUREK

Rosen
YA™
New York

Published in 2019 by The Rosen Publishing Group, Inc.
29 East 21st Street, New York, NY 10010

Copyright © 2019 by The Rosen Publishing Group, Inc.

First Edition

Library of Congress Cataloging-in-Publication Data

Names: Mazurek, John, author.
Title: The road to marriage equality / John Mazurek.
Description: New York : Rosen Publishing, 2019. | Series: The history of the LGBTQ+ rights movement | Includes bibliographical references and index. | Audience: Grades 7–12.
Identifiers: LCCN 2017030244 | ISBN 9781538381328 (library bound) | ISBN 9781508183105 (pbk.)
Subjects: LCSH: Same-sex marriage—United States—History—Juvenile literature. | Gay rights—United States—History—Juvenile literature.
Classification: LCC HQ1034.U5 P37 2018 | DDC 306.84/80973—dc23
LC record available at https://lccn.loc.gov/2017030244

Manufactured in the United States of America

On the cover: Protestors carry signs during a November 15, 2008, march in San Francisco opposing a California statewide ban on same-sex marriage (*top*). Amber Weiss (*left*) and Sharon Papo (*right*) stand outside the San Francisco City Hall in June 2008 ahead of their marriage ceremony (*bottom*).

CONTENTS

INTRODUCTION

L GBTQ+ history has many compartments. Every different type of member of the community has a unique set of needs, and they share a unique history of oppression. Different types of communities under the queer umbrella have sometimes conflicted with each other and acted against the other's interests, but that's not to say that they have never worked together.

The topic of same-sex marriage is one that is particular to gay people and other people who have same-sex attraction that they might want to express in the institution of marriage. As such, victories and defeats in the name of same-sex marriage haven't changed the capabilities of asexual individuals, transgender people, or other communities that don't necessarily identify as holding same-sex attraction. This means that straight asexuals and transgender people would likely be acting as allies when focusing on issues to do with marriage equality unless

On June 26, 2015, marriage equality supporters erupt into cheers after the US Supreme Court ruled that bans against same-sex marriage were unconstitutional.

they had an invested interest that offered them the direct benefit of gaining a right.

Marriage is an institution that many people view as the ultimate commitment between two partners, but it is also a legal institution that confers rights and protections. That is why for most of American history, same-sex partners had been denied something far greater than a piece of paper when they were turned away from their attempts to receive a marriage license. To be denied marriage also meant to be denied protections that included the right to exist as a family unit, the right to make legal decisions as a parent or spouse, and the right to self-govern one's family in a way that is agreeable to the law.

The road to marriage equality from 1990 to the present is the story of what it was like to live in a country where one could pay taxes, vote, or even risk one's life for one's nation by serving in the military and still be treated like a second-class citizen. The story is not a single narrative that is composed of a clear beginning, middle, and end. It is instead composed of hundreds of stories, court cases, protests, legal battles, and pieces of legislation that are indelibly intertwined and connected to the larger idea of equality.

Although discrimination remains a harmful facet of being a queer person in America, many actors have taken great strides over the last three decades to secure basic civil liberties. The progress can be measured as such: In 1990, many American citizens did not believe it was possible that they might someday live in a country where they could marry a same-sex partner. Yet, *Obergefell v. Hodges* made that reality possible in 2015, long enough after the story's beginning that some who fought for marriage equality over the decades never saw it federally mandated. Still, many fights lie ahead for the LGBTQ+ community because no victory is guaranteed to last.

CHAPTER ONE

THE NEW CAMPAIGN

· ·

M embers of the LGBTQ+ community faced major roadblocks in the fight for equality, civil rights, and acceptance at the start of the 1990s. Violence, routine discrimination in both public and private sectors of life, and lack of representation in media and the government were often awaiting the opportunity to afflict queer individuals and whole communities with some crisis. The conservative backlash that followed the AIDS crisis of the 1980s further complicated the liberation movement on a national scale.

In contrast, during the years leading up to 1992, the fight for same-sex marriage and equality at large had only witnessed a few strides forward. Civil rights for sexual minorities in particular began to find increasing public and vocal support in pockets across the country. The conversation, itself, eventually gained enough traction to become a central issue in the 1992 presidential election.

SYSTEMIC VIOLENCE AND PUBLIC OPINION

On April 28, 1990, a pipe bomb consisting of three firecrackers exploded inside of Uncle Charlie's, a West Village bar in New York City frequented by members of the LGBTQ+ community. Three people were injured and dozens of patrons rushed into the street in a panic.

In the early 1990s, the rate of hate crimes continued to skyrocket across the country, and both state and federal law provided little protection for its targets. The Hate Crime Statistics Act of 1990, signed into law by President George H. W. Bush, urged for better reporting of hate-based crimes by the Federal Bureau of Investigation (FBI), but at that time, federal hate crime laws failed to recognize gender or sexual orientation as motivating factors for violence, which often resulted in the underreporting of crimes by victims. The government thus held an indifferent attitude toward the fact of hate crimes as gendered or heteronormative violence.

Advocates, organizations, and individual states therefore had to create their own systems of reporting and accountability in order to publicize and combat violence. One such organization, the New York City Gay and Lesbian Anti-Violence Project, shed light on the severity of this issue. They revealed that the number of reported antigay crimes increased from 308 to 507 between 1989 and 1990 in New York City alone.

Protestors gather outside of Borough Hall in Brooklyn, New York, on February 2, 1990. They are drawing attention to the death of James Zappalorti, a man who was killed in an act of antigay violence.

This political and social backdrop existed in the realm of the general public's opinion of LGBTQ+ people. Data gleaned from a number of surveys conducted by the General Social Survey (GSS) confirms that the overall public opinion toward LGBTQ+ people in the early 1990s was largely mixed. When survey participants were asked whether or not an openly gay man should be allowed to teach at a college or university, a majority of those interviewed in both 1990 and 1991 responded that he should be allowed. Yet, when participants were asked whether sexual relations between members of the same sex were wrong, survey takers in 1990 and 1991 overwhelmingly responded that it was "always wrong."

Public opinion highlighted how difficult gaining support for marriage equality would be because many people were still uncomfortable with or adjusting to the idea of LGBTQ+ people having equal rights and treatment under the law and in society. These questions from the survey alone show that considerations of equal rights seemed to center around people's judgment of the community instead of an evaluation of the community's basic needs. Still, activists and allies around the country continued to push forward with efforts to advocate for legislation that would lay the groundwork for marriage equality.

DOMESTIC PARTNERSHIPS AS AN INROAD TOWARD MARRIAGE

Baker v. Nelson (1972) set the precedent for denying same-sex couples the right to marry. In that case, the federal government made it clear that same-sex marriage was an issue for the state to decide and not the federal government. As a result of these restrictions, many same-sex couples realized that the battleground for marriage had to take place on a state-by-state basis. Fifty battles meant a long and difficult road ahead.

And there was much that same-sex partners had to win. Excluding same-sex couples from the institution of marriage meant they didn't have access to certain legal protections that married people were entitled to, including tax breaks, inheritance, and medical guardianship.

In order to legally circumvent bans on same-sex marriage and to gain access to some relationship rights and protections, many same-sex couples began to look toward domestic partnerships as solutions that offered some degree of marriage equality. Domestic partnerships, or a legal relationship between two unmarried partners, could offer individuals a low level of protection that varied from state to state, county to county, and even city to city. Yet, domestic partnerships still afforded non-married partners privileges they previously could not access, such as hospital visitation and the ability to get coverage on a partner's health insurance plan. While not being fully holistic, these gains in protections were important steps toward equality under the law in the 1990s.

In 1989, Mayor Art Agnos of San Francisco signed a bill for a same-sex domestic partnership registry, but it was narrowly repealed by the voters. A watered down version that offered no protections was passed in November 1990, taking effect on Valentine's Day the following year. Despite not offering protections, the registry served as a symbolic catalog for many that validated a type of same-sex union in the eyes of the law. As Terry Jentry, who registered his relationship, said on opening day, "We are doing this because we think it should be legal (to marry). This shows we have more of a commitment. It is a statement that if

Governor William Weld of Massachusetts speaks with a reporter at a press conference on July 10, 1991. He is holding the state budget he had just signed.

things don't work out we are not going to run away."
In 1992, the governor of Massachusetts, William
Weld, signed an executive order that allowed
state employees in Massachusetts to register as
domestic partners, granting them bereavement
leave as well as hospital and prison visitations.

Domestic partnerships soon became a
contentious issue in the United States as more and
more same-sex couples began to push for equal
benefits and privileges equal to or beyond domestic
partnerships. However, the movement to fight for
legalization of domestic partnerships did not gain
strong momentum until the 2000s.

THE HUMAN RIGHTS CAMPAIGN ENDORSES BILL CLINTON

Money has played a large role in shaping American
policy and politics for many years. Groups called
political action committees (PACs) are often at the
heart of influencing policy.

In the 1980s, conservative PACs such as Moral
Majority led by the conservative Baptist minister
Jerry Falwell mobilized many conservative Christians
to support candidates who had heteronormative
platforms. If elected, those candidates would
significantly damage the legal pathways to civil
rights for the sexual minority and transgender
community.

KAREN THOMPSON AND SPOUSAL RIGHTS

Karen Thompson was in a four-year relationship with Sharon Kowalski when Thompson found herself in the midst of a heated spousal rights battle. Thompson and Kowalski could not legally be married because they were a same-sex couple, but they lived in a house together, exchanged wedding bands, and considered themselves life partners.

In 1983, Kowalski sustained brain damage and was rendered quadriplegic in a car accident. After the accident, the state awarded guardianship to Kowalski's parents because Thompson was not her legal spouse and therefore was not allowed to make medical decisions or have custody of her. To make matters worse, Kowalski's parents barred Thompson from seeing her upon learning about their relationship.

After a seven-year legal battle, the state awarded Thompson guardianship in 1991, but not before numerous appeals. William Rubenstein, director of the American Civil Liberties Union's Lesbian and Gay Rights Project, concisely summarized the heartbreaking reality that people in same-sex relationships regularly faced because of legal discrimination: "This case exemplifies the difficulties lesbians and gay men have in safeguarding our relationships. The remarkable thing about this case is not that Karen Thompson finally won guardianship, but that it took her seven years to do so, when guardianship rights for a heterosexual married couple would be taken for granted."

In response, pro-LGBTQ+ political action organizations began to form in order to lobby for rights and protections. The Human Rights Campaign Fund (HRC), a PAC founded 1980 by Steve Endean, quickly became one of the largest and most influential mainstream LGBTQ+ organizations. Its size and influence allowed it to hold unprecedented power to lobby for a community.

In 1989, the HRC restructured by overhauling its mission and function and dropped the word "Fund" from its name. It began to focus its energies on educating the public and providing resources for

This June 17, 2017, photo shows the Human Rights Campaign office in Washington, DC. The organization is honoring the forty-nine victims of the Pulse nightclub shooting in Orlando, Florida.

the lesbian, gay, and bisexual (LGB) community. It also started procuring funds for media outreach and lobbying for social welfare. These changes were in addition to its usual PAC activities. In 1992, the HRC endorsed a presidential candidate, Bill Clinton, for the first time, making him the first president to be supported by an LGB organization.

TRANSPHOBIA WITHIN THE LGBTQ+ MOVEMENT

Historically, many members of the transgender community took issue with various queer/gay liberation efforts and organizations such as the HRC for two reasons: transgender exclusion and elitism.

Sylvia Rivera, a transgender activist of Puerto Rican and Venezuelan descent, fought fervently for the queer community by championing a New York City Transgender Rights Bill and acting as a founding member of the Gay Liberation Front (GLF). But her eventual dismissal from the GLF created division and resentment.

Another cause of resentment was subsequent decisions to exclude transgender individuals from mainstream efforts to gain civil rights protections

Sylvia Rivera stands at the head of ACT UP during the 1994 Pride March in New York City. The yearly commemoration of the Stonewall uprising always shines a litght on ongoing LGBTQ+ struggles.

through lobbying and legislative efforts. One such decision to exclude transgender people's needs occurred during Elizabeth Birch's tenure as the HRC director from 1995 to 2004. The HRC opposed including transgender rights in EDNA, a piece of legislation aimed at fighting discrimination. Such actions made the schism between transgender activists and the mainstream gay liberation movement all the more apparent.

As 1992 drew closer, for the first time in American history, the topic of the rights of sexual minorities was being debated on a national scale. While incumbent George H. W. Bush distanced himself from any discussion concerning LGBTQ+ rights, democratic nominee Bill Clinton carefully explored his relationship with the queer community by making campaign promises to address workplace equality. At the time, no laws were in place to protect an employee's right to work free of discrimination based on their sexual orientation. Clinton also vowed to overturn the 1981 ban on lesbians and gays in the armed services.

Many accused the Arkansas governor with co-opting a popular social issue in order to appeal to voters. Regardless of reservations many had about the authenticity of Clinton's ability to champion civil rights during his term in the White House, advocates were excited by the prospects that Clinton outlined in his platform. His presidential win on November 3, 1992, signaled for many people a hopeful future.

CHAPTER TWO

BILLS, BILLS, BILLS

· ·

The military became the place where another form of overt sexual- and gender-based discrimination emerged. A policy called Don't Ask, Don't Tell changed the conversation on how policymakers talked about and tackled discrimination on a federal level. From there, several pieces of legislation denied or offered protections for those affected by discrimination stemming from their sexual or gender identities. Many policies introduced during this era laid the groundwork for the legislative paths toward equality in marriage and protections in the workplace and in hiring practices.

DON'T ASK, DON'T TELL

Before taking office in 1992, President-elect Bill Clinton conveyed his wish to lift the ban on gays and lesbians serving in the armed forces. Clinton's campaign promise, however, was at odds with the very people in positions to implement the move, including generals such as Colin Powell. Democrats in key positions, such as chairman of the US Senate Committee on Armed Services Sam Nunn, argued against it. They claimed that morale would be negatively affected by the mere presence of gay servicemen and servicewomen.

Ultimately, Clinton was unable to lift the ban completely and settled for a compromise measure called DADT. Under this policy, gay and bisexual individuals could work in the armed forces if they did not openly declare their sexual orientation. Further, those who might question service members' sexuality were discouraged from such inquiries.

President Bill Clinton, shown here on March 19, 1993, had to compromise with DADT, under which gay and bisexual soldiers could serve if they kept their sexual orientation a secret.

A Pew Research survey conducted in July 1994, five months after DADT was signed into law, found that 52 percent of Americans supported the new law while 45 percent opposed permitting gays and lesbians to serve openly. DADT was unpopular with military leaders who felt that the policy did not do enough to expel LGB service members from active service. It was also a devastating blow to many LGB activists who supported Clinton's initial pledge and voted for him in 1992 based on it. Although DADT was introduced as a liberalizing policy, many LGB rights activists argued that the measure forced soldiers into secrecy and encouraged further discrimination. It turns out that they weren't wrong. By 2008, fifteen years after the policy had been adopted, more than twelve thousand officers had been discharged for refusing to hide their sexual orientation.

EDNA AND THE REPUBLICAN REVOLUTION

President Clinton also led many LGB individuals to believe that his administration would enact federal protections against sexual orientation discrimination through new legislation. The Employment Non-Discrimination Act (ENDA) was an attempt to do just that. Introduced in 1994 during Clinton's first term, the bill prohibited discrimination against employees based on their sexual orientation in workplaces that employed fifteen or more people. But ENDA did not

This is a January 1995 photo of Gerry Studds, a US senator from Massachusetts. He was the first openly gay member of Congress. Although it never passed, he was the one who introduced the Employee Non-Discrimination Act.

address gender identity and offered no protections for transgender individuals.

ENDA never saw the light of day as a law. Despite its defeat in 1994, ENDA was revised on multiple occasions in the coming years and was introduced to Congress and defeated again and again over the next two decades.

Frustrated by the lack of forward momentum on the bill, Clinton sidestepped the congressional voting process in 1998 by signing an executive order prohibiting federal employees from being discriminated against due to their sexual orientation. Although this did little to advance the original goal of the bill and to protect people employed by the private sector, it was a small step in the right direction.

Missteps during Clinton's first term soured public opinion and alienated many voters. The Whitewater investigation, the continued debate over Clinton's health care initiative, and the inability to pass a budget without the federal government plunging into deficit spending resulted in Democrats losing control of both houses of Congress during the 1994 midterm elections. This was the first time in forty years that Republicans controlled both houses. The years that followed were labeled as the Republican Revolution and featured Senator Newt Gingrich presiding over the House with an adversarial attitude that had rarely been displayed in Washington politics before that time.

As Congress clashed over funding issues, efforts to pass newer versions of ENDA stymied.

The 1996 proposal of ENDA narrowly lost on a 49–50 vote in the Senate and was never voted on in the House. With Newt Gingrich and conservatives dominating Congress and an electorate still uneasy and unaccustomed to the questions of sexual orientation, the headwinds had slowly turned against the fight for LGBTQ+ awareness and equality under the law.

BAEHR V. LEWIN

In 1993, a case by the name of In *Baehr v. Lewin*, which later became known as *Baehr v. Miike*, made national headlines. Three same-sex couples filed discrimination suits against the Department of Public Health in Honolulu when they were denied wedding licenses because of the state's ban on same-sex marriage.

The Hawaii Supreme Court agreed to hear the case. Thousands of allies and advocates for LGBTQ+ rights across the country held their breath. If Hawaii set a precedent for legalizing same-sex marriage, then there was a good chance that other states would follow suit.

The court ruled that the state ban violated the plaintiffs' constitutional rights. But it wasn't over yet. The Hawaii Supreme Court sent the case back to the

(continued on the next page)

(continued from the previous page)

lower courts to give the state the chance to justify discriminating against same-sex couples.

This time, the trial court also ruled against the state. Opponents of same-sex marriage regarded these developments in favor of marriage equality as a hostile invasion on "traditional family values." While the Hawaii Supreme Court was in the process of considering the state's appeal, conservative opponents organized and funded a political campaign that led to the citizens of Hawaii passing a constitutional amendment that nullified the claim of the same-sex couples. Because of that last development, the Hawaii Supreme Court ruled in favor of the state, and against marriage equality.

The conservative backlash didn't end there. This case set into motion the last of the successful onslaughts of state and federal anti-marriage equality legislation in the history of the United States.

By 2006, California, Hawaii, Maine, and Washington, DC, permitted only domestic partnerships between same-sex partners. Many other states explicitly prohibited same-sex marriage.

Same-sex marriage laws

New Jersey's governor has signed a law making civil unions for gay couples legal. It is the third state to allow civil unions.

Current state laws

■ Prohibit same-sex marriage*

■ Allow domestic partnerships (limited marriage rights)

▨ Permit civil unions (give gay couples many of same benefits, protections as married couples)

☐ Permit same-sex marriage

☐ No state law

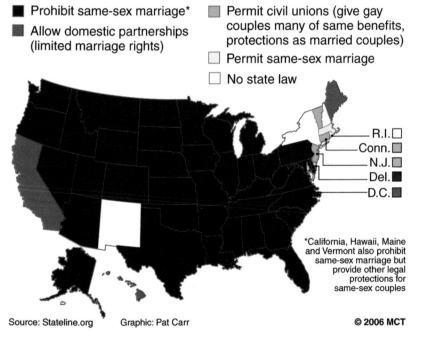

R.I. ☐
Conn. ▨
N.J. ▨
Del. ■
D.C. ■

*California, Hawaii, Maine and Vermont also prohibit same-sex marriage but provide other legal protections for same-sex couples

Source: Stateline.org   Graphic: Pat Carr

© 2006 MCT

THE PASSING OF DOMA

Despite the conservative outrage in response to *Baehr v. Miike* and an increasingly unfriendly political climate, many same-sex marriage advocates clung onto the hope that the right legal battles would set the conditions in motion for marriage equality. This hope was crippled in 1996. In response to *Baehr*, many states began to introduce state constitutional bans barring same-sex marriage to curb any similar lawsuits from going into effect. Soon after, one of the most damaging pieces of anti-LGBT legislation in years passed in the federal arena of Washington, DC.

Until this point, the federal government had no definition of marriage. Conservative organizations began to point to same-sex marriage as the most imminent threat to traditional family values in history. Politicians and lawmakers from both the Democratic and Republican parties were not ready to embrace the idea of same-sex marriage either. They began to look for ways to curb any momentum for marriage equality. President Clinton, despite moving some LGBTQ+ civil rights issues forward, was also adamant about opposing same-sex marriage. He stated during an interview with *The Advocate*, "I believe that marriage is an institution for the union of a man and a woman." Clinton even avoided answering whether legal protections should be given to domestic partners in same-sex unions.

It wasn't surprising, then, when Representative Bob Barr (R-GA) introduced to Congress a bill colloquially called the Defense of Marriage Act (DOMA) in 1996. The bill restricted the official, federal definition of marriage to that of a man and a woman. It also allowed states to ban same-sex marriage in their constitutions and legalized a state's ability to ignore any same-sex marriage conducted in another state. Additionally, DOMA denied same-sex couples over one thousand federal protections that a marriage provided. Some protections denied to those who weren't allowed to marry included access to a partner's employment benefits, rights of inheritance, the ability to file joint tax returns, immigration or residency for noncitizen partners, domestic abuse protection, and next-of-kin status. Supporters of DOMA argued that same-sex marriage promoted alternative family formations and promiscuity. They also stated that the basis for marriage was procreation, an act that was considered elusive to those in same-sex relationships. Opponents argued that DOMA discriminated on the basis of sex and conflated homosexuality with incest and polygamy.

DOMA quickly passed in both the House of Representatives (342–67) and the Senate (85–14) with a huge majority. President Bill Clinton sealed the deal by choosing to sign the bill into law instead of vetoing it.

These were difficult times for the millions who wanted to marry and enjoy the same status their straight counterparts took for granted. DADT, ENDA,

Jack Baker (*left*) and Michael McConnell (*right*) were among the few who managed to marry during the early fight for marriage equality. They obtained a marriage license in 1971 in Blue Earth County, Minnesota.

and DOMA wove discrimination based on sexual identity into the federal legislation explicitly and made the ongoing battle for equality and civil rights largely uphill.

LGBTQ+ advocates of the early 1990s, however, had much to be proud of and much to look forward to. They succeeded in getting Americans to talk about sexual orientation on the national stage and made legislative strides toward demanding equality under the law with regard to marriage and discrimination. These themes continued playing an important role in the latter half of the decade as the public tide turned in favor of LGBTQ+ representation.

CHAPTER THREE

NEW AVENUES FOR CHANGE: ACTION IN THE STATES

I n 1996, only 27 percent of Americans felt that same-sex marriage should be legalized. In line with public opinion were politicians who were in a position to make change. In fact, political opposition to same-sex marriage was bipartisan: 33 percent of Democrats supported recognizing same-sex marriage as a legal institution, while just 17 percent of Republicans were in favor of it. The lack of support in Washington meant that marriage equality advocates had to enact change at the state level. But opponents of same-sex marriage were eager to work against them.

ALASKA SUPREME COURT RESPONDS TO BAEHR

Alaska led efforts to restrict the definition of marriage even before DOMA was enacted. In February 1996, the Alaska House of Representatives passed a bill narrowing the definition of marriage to a union between one man and one woman. State Senator Lyda Green

Supporters of same-sex marriage rally outside of the federal courthouse in Anchorage, Alaska, on October 10, 2014. This was days before a judge declared Alaska's ban unconstitutional.

introduced a bill restricting marriage even further, to a "civil contract between one man and one woman." The particularly restrictive addition her bill offered was that it would forbid the state from recognizing same-sex marriages performed outside Alaska. Green's bill also stated that marriage benefits would not apply to same-sex couples in Alaska. Green's bill became law by default without the signature of Governor Tony Knowles.

In February 1998, the Alaska Supreme Court ruled that the choice of one's partner in marriage is a "fundamental right," and that the state must show "compelling reason" why marriage must be limited to opposite-sex couples and why same-sex couples should not receive the same benefits.

Responding to the Court's decision, Alaska voters passed a ballot amendment to the state's constitution narrowing the definition of marriage to opposite-sex couples. A similar ballot initiative in Hawaii passed in November.

A MURDER INSPIRES TOLERANCE

On a cold October night in 1998 on the outskirts of Laramie, Wyoming, twenty-one-year-old Matthew Shepard was beaten, tied to a fence, and left to die. He remained there for eighteen hours before he was brought to a hospital. He died five days later.

The murder sparked demonstrations across the country and reactions worldwide. The young man's death became a symbol of the need for hate crimes legislation. Although federal laws covered hate crimes based on race, national origin, and religion, no laws covered hate crimes motivated by sexual orientation. And, Wyoming was one of ten states that had no hate crime laws covering specific categories of people. However, it was a long journey before a strong, national law was enacted.

GLAAD, formerly the Gay and Lesbian Alliance Against Defamation, was one such group that

STONEWALL INN ENTERS HISTORY

Stonewall Inn, site of the Stonewall Uprising, is considered by many the most important site of the LGBTQ+ liberation movement. Thanks to the efforts of GLAAD, the Greenwich Village Society for Historic Preservation, and the Association of Gay and Lesbian Architects and Designers, the National Register of Historic Places (NRHP) declared Stonewall Inn a National Historic Landmark in 2000. This placed Stonewall in the ranks of such iconic places as Independence Hall and the battlefield where the Battle of Wounded Knee occurred. NRHP recognition meant that Stonewall Inn, long a symbol of violent resistance against a legal system that discriminated against sexual orientation, was now officially accepted as part of the national identity.

worked to change this environment. It was founded in New York City in 1985 as a response to sensationalized reporting during the AIDS epidemic. The goal was to put pressure on media outlets to end homophobic reporting. After a 1987 meeting with GLAAD, the *New York Times* began to use the word "gay" instead of more offensive words.

By the 1990s, chapters of GLAAD had opened in major cities nationwide. In March 1993, GLAAD organized a massive turnout of same-sex couples on the first day of domestic partnership registration in New York City. Following the murder of Shepard, GLAAD activists went to Laramie to conduct vigils and facilitate a national dialogue on hate crimes that targeted sexual minorities. GLAAD's efforts to promote fair depictions of members of the LGBTQ+ community in journalism and entertainment and its promotion of the idea that hate crimes can be perpetrated based on one's sexual orientation have done well to fulfill the goal of educating the public via discourse.

While GLAAD was making people aware of hate crimes, other organizations began to change their attitudes independently. One remarkable example is the Central Conference of American Rabbis (CCAR), the largest and oldest rabbinical organization in the world. CCAR was the first major religious organization to recognize same-sex unions. The "Resolution on Same

Actor and comedian Orlando Jones arrives at a GLAAD-sponsored screening of the TV series *American Gods*. GLAAD's mission is to promote positive portrayals of LGBTQ+ people.

Gender Officiation" was passed at the 111th CCAR convention, in March 2000, offering the protection of Reform Judaism to clergy who officiate same-sex unions. At a time when Christian denominations

Rabbis Paul Menitoff, Charles A. Kroloff, Denise Eger, Shira Stern, and Susan B. Stone discuss the decision to allow clerical participation in same-sex ceremonies during a press conference in North Carolina.

were censoring and prohibiting clergy who officiated same-sex marriages, CCAR's 1,800 Reform rabbis saw themselves as a counterweight and hoped other faith groups would follow.

However, not all wings of Judaism agreed with CCAR's paradigm shift. Within Jewish opposition, many critics cite the Torah, which calls homosexuality an abomination. Nevertheless, CCAR's actions represented a substantial group with significant clout in the sphere of public opinion. Their move to include same-sex couples in marriage rites was one that no other major religious organization was willing to make at the turn of the century.

VEERING FROM ACCEPTANCE TO INTOLERANCE AROUND THE STATES

Vermont explored same-sex legislation early in 2000. The intention was to establish that marriage was restricted to one man and one woman, but also to extend the same legal protections to civil unions that marriage unions enjoyed. State politicians leaned toward guaranteeing equal rights and benefits to same-sex couples in civil unions. By April, it became a reality: this piece of legislation had been signed into law in Vermont.

Just seven months later, Nebraska began work on the most sweeping ban on same-sex marriage yet. The ballot measure banned not only same-sex marriage but also invalidated every other union not meeting the state's narrow definition of marriage. Some unions that it invalidated were domestic partnerships and civil unions.

Opponents worried that the amendment would convince employers and insurers not to offer health benefits to same-sex couples. Opponents also feared that the amendment would be interpreted by hospitals or government agencies to mean that same-sex partners could not make decisions regarding their spouse's children or, if hospitalized, their medical decisions.

Supporters of the Nebraska amendment worried that the Vermont legislation would jeopardize the traditional definition of marriage. Nebraska was responding to the *Baehr* decision just as Alaska

Gray Davis, who served as California's governor from 1999 to 2003, gave same-sex couples in California the right to make health care decisions for their partners. He also fought against sexual orientation discrimination in the judicial system.

had in 1998 because Nevada residents were voting for or against defining marriage in the state's constitution to eliminate same-sex couples. It passed by a margin of 70 percent in favor and 29 percent opposed.

The tide against same-sex marriage was swelling even in liberal coastal states. In 1999, California Governor Gray Davis approved the first-ever state registry for domestic partnerships and ended the state's de facto ban on gay adoption. When Davis left office in 2003, domestic partnership in California had leaped ahead of the rest of the country. A domestic partnership registry with broad protections for same-sex couples was a remarkable victory after the setbacks in Alaska, Hawaii, and Nebraska. However, in March 2000, Californians passed Proposition 22, which said that California would only recognize marriages between one man and one woman. It passed by a wide margin, 61 percent in favor and just 38 percent opposed, and its success surprised many. It meant that people in California supported granting same-sex couples some legal protection through domestic partnerships, but that marriage was still off-limits.

CHAPTER FOUR

MAJOR MILESTONES

T he new century ushered in LGBTQ+ awareness in popular culture as well as in political discourse. Public support for including same-sex couples in marriage, tepid during the 1990s, began to increase, especially among the millennial generation just entering the political scene. Most Americans, however, still regarded marriage in the traditional sense, and conservative lawmakers used same-sex marriage as a wedge to split conservatives and moderates from the liberal voting base.

MAINSTREAM PORTRAYALS OF LGBTQ+ PEOPLE

The late 1990s and early 2000s saw many more representations of LGBTQ+ people in the mainstream media and in culture than ever before. Ellen DeGeneres famously came out on her primetime show and in an interview with Oprah in 1997 at a time when public figures were hesitant to reveal their sexual orientation for fear

Author and activist Urvashi Vaid has worked for organizations such as the American Civil Liberties Union (ACLU), the Center for Gender and Sexuality Law at Columbia Law School, and the National Gay and Lesbian Task Force (NGLTF).

of being blacklisted or admonished. Her coming out created what many people consider a starter spark in mainstream culture. By the mid-2000s, actors such as Neil Patrick Harris, George Takei, and Rosie O'Donnell had publicly disclosed their sexual orientation and began to advocate openly for LGBTQ+ rights. Although derogatory stereotypes of queer identities continued to pollute popular media in both film and TV, the cultural shift in visibility for real queer people had an even greater impact.

Literature also gave the LGBTQ+ community space to advocate for and publicize the goals of the equality movement in a way that allowed for mass dissemination. Urvashi Vaid's 2002 book, *Virtual Equality: The Mainstreaming of Gay and Lesbian Liberation,* provided a concise insight into the goals and stumbling blocks on the road to equality. Vaid, a lifelong activist, highlighted the irony of certain political paradoxes that bred inequality and discrimination, such as the fact that LGBTQ+ people paid taxes yet failed to receive protection from the government. Her book, along with hundreds of other manifestos and memoirs, created a visibility that lent the LGBTQ+ community increasing understanding and acceptance within the cultural sphere.

LAWRENCE V. TEXAS

Until 2003, antisodomy laws and homosexual conduct statutes criminalized consensual sexual relations between same-sex partners. Same-sex partners were often arrested, fined, or even charged with a felony for merely being intimate with a partner. These prohibitions not only violated privacy and freedom but also endangered and penalized thousands of individuals by equating a non-criminal activity such as consensual sex with violent crimes such as rape and murder. The fight to end such discriminatory practices was an extremely important stepping stone that paved a legal pathway for equality and marriage.

Bowers v. Hardwick was the first attempt to overturn antisodomy laws in a federal court of law. The case, which was presented to the Supreme Court in 1986, argued that antisodomy laws violated a person's constitutional rights. That argument was shot down in a 5–4 verdict, with the majority stating that the Constitution did not outline fundamental rights in regard to homosexuality.

In the years that followed, many states loosened their enforcement of antisodomy laws or repealed them altogether, but same-sex intimacy was still considered illegal in fourteen states by the time *Lawrence v. Texas*

Tyron Gardener (*left*) and John Lawrence (*right*), the petitioners of *Lawrence v. Texas*, appear before supporters and media after their court victory in 2003.

was presented to the Supreme Court in 2003. The petitioners, supported by the gay rights advocacy organization Lambda Legal, successfully argued that antisodomy laws violated the Fourteenth Amendment, which guarantees American citizens equal protection under the law. In a 6–3 verdict, the Supreme Court overruled *Bowers v. Hardwick,* making same-sex intimacy a constitutional right in the United States. Justice Anthony Kennedy delivered the majority opinion of the Court, stating that, "The State cannot demean their [the petitioners'] existence or control their destiny by making their private sexual conduct a crime."

National reactions were mixed at the time of the decision. Many conservatives and religious organizations were outraged by what they considered a violation of family values. Progressives were glad that the argument of equal protection was affirmed.

MASSACHUSETTS AND SAN FRANCISCO PAVE THE WAY

Up until 2003, civil unions acted as a sometimes-incomplete substitute put in place by many states to appease or stall momentum toward fully realized marriage equality. Marriage, as it was defined federally and within individual states, remained a union between two people of the opposite sex. However, the landmark case *Goodridge v. Department of Public Health* in November 2003 changed the trajectory of marriage equality and marked a huge victory and turning point. Representing seven same-sex couples who were denied marriage licenses, GLAAD sued the Massachusetts Department of Public Health and challenged the idea that marriage was an institution that has the sole purpose of reproduction. In a 4–3 decision, the Massachusetts Supreme Judicial Court overturned the state ban on same-sex marriage and stated that "barring an individual from the protections, benefits, and obligations of civil marriage solely because that person would marry a person of the same sex violates the Massachusetts Constitution." By May of the following year, Massachusetts became the first state to issue marriage certificates to same-sex couples and grant the benefits of marriage to them.

The city of San Francisco quickly followed suit when, in 2004, the mayor announced that the city was going to defy California state law and issue marriage certificates for same-sex couples. Thousands of couples flooded city hall to have the city recognize their unions. Within a month of the declaration, however, the state of California annulled all marriages performed and charged the mayor with a breach of the law. This brief period became called California's "Winter of Love."

Much like this, the road to federally legalized same-sex marriage continued to morph over the next decade. However, the actions passed in Massachusetts and steps taken in San Francisco signaled something very important: they provided a basis for a challenge to the constitutionality of DOMA and gave other states precedents to reference when their own battles began.

STATES TAKE ON MARRIAGE EQUALITY

The period between 2004 and 2006 saw a sharp increase in legislation aimed at banning same-sex marriage on a state-by-state basis, federally, and even constitutionally in response to *Goodridge.* George W. Bush, the incumbent president who was ramping up for re-election in November 2008, felt pressure from his conservative constituents to discourage increasing calls for marriage equality by championing the Federal Marriage Amendment (FMA), a proposed amendment to the Constitution that would define marriage as a union between a man and a woman. Between 2002 and 2006, the amendment was introduced to Congress five times. Passing it required majority support that it never received.

Although the proposed amendment to the US Constitution lacked enough support to be instated, many conservatives began to look for ways to curb what they perceived as an attack on traditional marriage in another way: amendments to state constitutions that proposed to ban same-sex marriage. They realized that individual states adopting amendments that barred same-sex marriage could more easily curtail any repeat performances of *Goodridge*. Adopting state amendments would also provide a stronger case for denial and/or recognition of same-sex marriages going forward.

Amendments that were passed varied in severity from state to state in the degree to which they refused to recognize same-sex unions. In South Dakota, for example, an amendment that banned same-sex marriage, civil unions, and domestic partnerships was passed. States like Oregon only banned same-sex marriage and recognized civil unions and domestic partnerships. By 2006, twenty-seven states had some form of state amendment banning same-sex marriage. The landscape and prospect of marriage equality thus became even murkier. In reaction, individual lawsuits brought up by LGB individuals continued to push against marriage discrimination. They didn't achieve much until 2008.

MILLENNIAL SUPPORT FOR SAME-SEX MARRIAGE

The Pew Research Center's annual polling of public opinion on major social issues showed a lukewarm upswing in support for same-sex marriage in the early 2000s. The number of those in favor rose from 32 percent in 2003 to 35 percent in 2006. Still, the general tenor of the country, both politically and publicly, was low support for the idea of openly embracing and demanding marriage equality during this period.

SOULFORCE AND EQUALITY RIDES

The Soulforce Ride of 2007 provides keen insight into how an increasing culture of acceptance challenged some conservatives of that time. Soulforce, an LGBTQ+ organization whose work aims to challenge the religious framework that oppresses the rights and livelihoods of the queer community, commissioned a series of non-violent demonstrations in the mid-2000s called Equality Rides. This format of demonstration took inspiration from Civil Rights-era Freedom Rides. Volunteers and allies traveled by bus to a series of conservative-leaning and religious colleges across the country in order to engage in a civil dialogue and discussion about gay rights.

Although they were often denied access or entry, the summer of rides sparked a national dialogue that highlighted the tension between the religious right and the progressive left. The rides also provided a relatively peaceful and public picture of the goals of the LGBTQ+ community aimed at working toward acceptance.

In 2006, Soulforce supporters participated in a march from the Colorado state capitol in Denver to the Focus on the Family headquarters in Colorado Springs to protest misrepresentation of the LGBTQ+ community.

However, interesting data began to surface suggesting that same-sex marriage was an issue that was generationally divisive. Data from the annual Pew Research Center's study called "Public Opinion on Same-Sex Marriage" shows a stark difference in support for marriage equality between the silent generation (1926–1945), baby boomers (1946–1964), Generation X (1965–1980), and millennials (1981 and later). In 2006, for instance, only 20 percent of the silent generation supported gay marriage. However, 50 percent of millennials were in favor of same-sex marriage. It seemed likely that LGBTQ+ equality would be a topic that was embraced and championed by younger generations that would soon have more agency in politics and culture.

CHAPTER FIVE

THE CHANGING TIDE

· ·

The environment that contributed to a paradigm shift in how Americans thought and responded to marriage equality was a diverse landscape. However, public opinion with respect to same-sex marriage changed dramatically during President Barack Obama's first term in office. In 2012, for the first time, the amount of Americans who supported legalizing same-sex marriage reached 50 percent. The efforts of LGBTQ+ advocates at the local, state, and federal levels were about to bear fruit with some help from the incoming president of the United States.

THE ROLLERCOASTER OF PROGRESS

The couples who had been married in California during the Winter of Love filed a lawsuit contesting the nullifications. The case eventually reached the California Supreme Court in 2008. The court ruled in favor of the couples. Its logic was that the state's ban of same-sex marriage was unconstitutional.

In response the court's decision, a series of conservative and religious organizations began a statewide campaign to get a measure called Proposition 8, or Prop 8, onto the 2008 state election ballot. The new proposition proposed to add restrictive language to the state constitution, saying, "only marriage between a man and a woman is valid or recognized in California."

The campaign to promote Proposition 8 was thorough. Thousands of advertising dollars and many minutes of airtime were devoted to the topic. Opponents fought just as fiercely by campaigning against the measure on social media and in popular culture. Nevertheless, the measure passed in November in a 52 to 48 percent vote, indicating that, slim as the margin was, the state was still not ready to embrace marriage equality.

Protests and lawsuits followed its passage into law. Three major lawsuits were filed within two weeks of the election's end. The plaintiffs argued that the amendment amounted to an unconstitutional revision of the state's charter. A coalition of activists, including GLAAD, the Human Rights Campaign, the California Teachers Association, and even the Pacific Gas and Electric Company donated money and time to influence the court to overturn the amendment. In May 2009, the California Supreme Court upheld the constitutionality of the amendment.

The grievance against the State of California was similar to *Baker v. Nelson*, in which the Minnesota Supreme Court ruled that the denial of marriage licenses to same-sex couples did not violate provisions of the United States Constitution. Baker's appeal eventually reached the United States Supreme Court. The court dismissed it on the basis that the appeal failed to raise a "substantial federal question." In dismissing Baker's appeal, the United States Supreme Court validated the notion that the responsibility for issuing marriage licenses and defining who qualifies for one is a matter for the states, not the federal government, to decide. *Baker* continued to play a role in establishing the precedent in future cases.

THE 2008 PRESIDENTIAL ELECTION

The 2008 presidential election proved to be a battleground for the two visions of marriage. State-level battles for and against marriage equality added extra fuel to the fire. The Republican Party platform reaffirmed the position that many conservatives held. The party hoped that electing frontrunner Senator John McCain to the presidency would ensure the future appointment of constitutionalist judges who would continue to preserve and champion the visions of "traditional" marriage and fight any attempts at repealing DOMA. McCain's position on LGBTQ+ rights was pretty hostile: he voted against ENDA in 1996, in favor of DOMA in 1996, and against repealing DADT. Yet he also voted against the FMA. These positions made it clear to the LGBTQ+ community that while McCain did not support same-sex marriage or LGBTQ+ rights, he might not assert federal powers to fight them.

Democrats also took a shaky stance toward marriage equality in their 2008 party platform.

Senator Barack Obama (*center*) of Illinois, who became the Democratic nominee in the 2008 presidential election, debates Republican nominee Senator John McCain (*right*).

Vague language such as support for the "full inclusion of gays and lesbians in the life of our nation," and a pledge to "seek equal responsibilities, benefits, and protections for these families" tried to sound inclusive without clearly

defining what institutions the Democratic Party approved LGBTQ+ people being a part of. Yet when it came to practically defining marriage equality on the federal level, the party took a careful stance by opposing DOMA but leaving it up to the states, not the federal government, to decide the legality of same-sex marriage. Democratic frontrunner Senator Barack Obama supported civil unions, not same-sex marriage. He also advocated for the repeal of DADT and DOMA. His position concerning what institutions to support for LGBTQ+ people evolved over his time in office after he won the election. The LGBTQ+

community supported his campaign in overwhelming numbers because they hoped that Obama would shift the national focus toward acceptance of same-sex unions and help to normalize the idea of equal protection under the law.

OBAMA'S ADVOCACY

While much of Obama's first term found him entrenched in an effort to save a failing economy, the president did make some serious moves that excited the LGBTQ+ community and allies. Obama appointed openly gay staff to various departments in the White House and expanded the benefits of federal employees who were in same-sex arrangements. In 2009, Obama also signed the Matthew Shepard and James Byrd, Jr., Hate Crimes Prevention Act, a law that allowed the federal government to charge someone with a hate crime if local or state enforcements failed to do so.

In 2007, the Local Law Enforcement Hate Crimes Prevention Act (also known as the Matthew Shepard Act) was introduced to address the gap in hate crime protections for LGBTQ+ people. The act was meant to expand 1969 United States federal hate-crime laws to include crimes motivated by the victim's real or perceived gender, sexual orientation, gender identity,

Justices Elena Kagan (*left*) and Sonia Sotomayor (*center*), both nominated to the Supreme Court by President Barack Obama, have often ruled in favor of upholding LGBTQ+ rights and protections.

or disability. Aside from the necessity of defining specific groups for protection under federal law, the law was deemed necessary because of the volume of hate crimes that sexual minorities and transgender people faced. According to Attorney General Eric Holder, the FBI had reported at least 77,000 hate crimes (presumably against the classes that were protected under the law) between the time of Matthew Shepard's death, in 1998, and when the resolution was introduced, in 2007. President Barack Obama signed the law in October 2009.

CONNECTICUT CUTS A NEW LINE

As the state of California was set to ban same-sex marriage, Connecticut was about to shake things up. The previous year, State Senator Andrew J. McDonald and State Representative Mike Lawlor submitted a bill that would give same-sex couples full marriage rights in the state of Connecticut. The bill passed a Judiciary Committee vote, but Governor Jodi Rell said she would veto any same-sex marriage legislation. Many residents of Connecticut at this time were also opposed to same-sex marriage. According to Quinnipiac University polls from 2004 and 2005, between 50 and 52 percent of residents opposed same-sex marriage. In April 2009, both the House and Senate agreed to replace all references to marriage with gender-neutral language and the governor signed the bill as revised. The law now read, "Marriage means the legal union of two persons." In this way, Connecticut became the second state, after Massachusetts, to recognize same-sex marriage.

In October 2010, the civil unions ended and all existing civil unions were converted to marriages. The state also recognized same-sex marriages, civil unions, and domestic partnerships officiated outside Connecticut. A same-sex couple could move to Connecticut and not worry that their marriage would be voided in the eyes of the law, and residents of Connecticut did not have to travel elsewhere to be married. Importantly, in voiding civil unions as an alternative to marriage, Connecticut underscored that the two were not actually equal institutions, though they might offer the same legal protections and benefits. This type of state level change challenged politicians and the public to think more critically about what marriage really meant to those involved and to society.

OBAMA AND THE DADT REPEAL

The year 2009 became highly influential for same-sex marriage thanks to efforts to amend state constitutions. Iowa became the third state to legalize same-sex marriage in April 2009. In May, the governor of Maine signed a bill legalizing same-sex marriage in that state. Maine was the first time a governor signed such a bill without being pressured by a court decision. In August, voters in Wisconsin approved a measure legalizing domestic partnerships for same-sex couples. In September, Vermont legalized same-sex marriage. In October, Nevada passed a law legalizing same-sex domestic partnerships. At the start of 2010, New Hampshire and the District of Columbia legalized same-sex marriage.

The major parties did little in 2009 to assist in the fight for marriage equality, but a surprising development was on the way in the form of a long-awaited appeal. In 2010, the Pentagon began a study of the effects of eliminating DADT in the military. In September of 2010, a federal judge ruled in favor of the plaintiffs in *Log Cabin Republicans v. United States of America*. And in November, the Pentagon released its findings: repeal of DADT would have little effect on the functioning of the military. In order to get around the congressional roadblocks that threatened a vote against the repeal, stand-alone "Don't Ask, Don't Tell" bills were released in the House and Senate in December. They each passed, and President Obama signed the bill into law on December 22. It officially took effect in September 2011.

OBAMA/ROMNEY 2012 PRESIDENTIAL CAMPAIGN

Since the 2008 presidential campaign, the cultural tide had changed in fundamental ways. In a sense, the public was moving faster on marriage equality than politicians in Washington. Public opinion was trending in a positive direction. According to Pew, 39 percent of Americans favored same-sex marriage in 2008. In 2012, that figure

On October 24, 2012, Paul Ryan (*left*) and Mitt Romney (*right*) part as they enter their campaign planes.

was 48 percent—a rise of nearly 10 percent in just four years.

In May 2012, President Obama announced that he was in favor of same-sex marriage. Obama thus became the first sitting president to give a thumbs-up to same-sex marriage. This reversed the position he laid out during the 2008 campaign: that marriage was a union of one man and one woman but that same-sex couples should receive the same legal protections without the title. Obama crossed a fine line by reiterating his heteronormative belief while also being open to the idea that same-sex couples could enjoy and participate in marriage in the same way as opposite-sex couples. This set him apart from his Republican opponent, Mitt Romney.

As the governor of Massachusetts, Romney opposed same-sex marriage. He fought all attempts to legalize it and opposed civil unions. When asked in an interview with the *Boston Globe* why he opposed civil unions while supporting domestic partnerships, Romney said, "If a civil union is identical to marriage other than in the name, I don't support that," he said. "But I certainly recognize that hospital visitation rights and benefits of that nature may well be appropriate. And states are able to make provisions for determination of those kinds of rights as well as, if you will, benefits that might accrue to state workers."

Some critics wondered if Obama's decision was political. Richard Grenell, an openly gay spokesperson for the US Mission to the United Nations under George W. Bush, summarized many sentiments of LGBTQ+ advocates and allies: "It's important to keep politicians from playing politics with a group's civil rights. The president's timing suggests that he is once again more concerned with his own political calculations than with actual equal rights." Grenell's point underscored the ambivalence of federal lawmakers on the issue of same-sex marriage. Despite having control of Congress and the executive branch for four years, Democrats in Washington were not making decisions based on morality. Instead, they seemed to be leading based on political expediency. That was about to change.

CHAPTER SIX

OVERTURNING DOMA AND THE LEGALIZATION OF SAME-SEX MARRIAGE

• •

B y the end of President Obama's first term in office, more Americans supported same-sex marriage than opposed it, and six states and the District of Columbia were performing same-sex marriages. States granting same-sex marriages were victories that came from local efforts to change state constitutions. DOMA still loomed large and defined marriage at the federal level. On a practical level, this federal designation superseded state constitutions and invalidated legal same-sex marriages in situations in which a same-sex spouse appealed to the federal government for some benefit. The only way to fight DOMA was by an act of Congress in Washington or by a ruling from the US Supreme Court.

KAREN GOLINSKI TAKES ON DOMA

One of the first cases against DOMA was filed by Karen Golinski, who sought to challenge the constitutionality of Section 3 of DOMA. Section

3 defined marriage federally as a union between one man and one woman. Golinski, a federal court employee of California, sought to add her spouse to her employer-provided health care plan. The judge ordered that Golinski be given family coverage after she filed a discrimination complaint in 2009. But the Office of Personnel Management (OPM), a federal agency, blocked those court orders and refused to allow Golinski to enroll her spouse for coverage. OPM claimed that DOMA prevented the agency from recognizing Golinski's marriage.

In 2010, Golinski filed suit against OPM to enforce the court order in a case known as *Golinski v. Office of Personnel Management*. US District Court Judge Jeffrey White dismissed the suit on procedural grounds and denied Golinski's request for an injunction. However, White left the door open for Golinski to argue against the constitutionality of OPM's denial of health benefits to a spouse under Section 3 of DOMA.

While Golinski was amending her lawsuit, US Attorney General Eric Holder announced that the US Department of Justice (DOJ) would no longer defend DOMA. However, the DOJ was still going to ensure that Congress had the opportunity to defend the law. The House of Representatives' Bipartisan Legal Advisory Group (BLAG) convened to defend DOMA in court by making appeals on behalf of the federal government. In February 2012, Judge White ruled in favor of Golinski by finding that Section 3 violated her right to equal protection under the Fifth Amendment. BLAG filed suit on behalf of DOMA.

This caused the case to go through a lengthy appeals process.

SUCCESSFULLY CHALLENGING DOMA THROUGH LAWSUITS

Two cases in Massachusetts made big waves when they challenged DOMA. The plaintiffs in *Gill v. Office of Personnel Management* were eight same-sex couples and three widowers who had all married in Massachusetts. In March 2009, they sued because government agencies had denied them benefits that had been granted to opposite-sex couples, including health benefits owed to a retired or deceased spouse, the ability to file income taxes as a married couple, and social security death benefit payments made to surviving spouses. They argued that Section 3 of DOMA was unconstitutional because the Fifth Amendment grants equal protection to everyone and because the federal government historically lets states decide the definition of marriage. In July 2010, US District Judge Joseph Tauro ruled in favor of the plaintiffs on the basis that Section 3 violated the equal protection clause of the Fifth Amendment. He found that Section 3 failed the rational basis review. This means that the government's argument defending Section 3 failed to define a compelling government interest that justified denying equal protection and due process. Just as occurred in *Golinski*, BLAG filed for appeal.

In July 2009, Attorney General of Massachusetts Martha Coakley filed a lawsuit challenging the constitutionality of Section 3 as well. Her challenge was that DOMA not only failed to offer equal protection, but that it also infringed on the state's right to determine how to define marriage. Judge Tauro, who also presided over that case, ultimately ruled that Section 3 did indeed violate the Tenth Amendment. Again, the DOJ and BLAG appealed the decisions and asked the United States Supreme Court not to pass judgments in *Gill* and *Golinski*.

However, the fight against DOMA was gaining momentum. Despite the efforts of the DOJ and BLAG to hinder further discussions, the 2013 case of *United States v. Windsor* dealt DOMA a final, fatal blow.

EDITH WINDSOR TAKES ON DOMA

Edith Windsor is best known for her role as the plaintiff in *United States v. Windsor*. Windsor met her long-term partner, Thea Spyer, in 1963, and the couple became engaged a few years later. With same-sex marriage remaining illegitimate in the eyes of the law, Windsor and Spyer remained unmarried despite their long relationship. When Spyer received a grim update on a heart condition, the couple decided to obtain a marriage in Canada in 2007.

Spyer died in 2009. This left Windsor with a $363,053 estate-tax bill on property that she inherited from Spyer. Since spouses aren't required to pay the estate tax, Windsor filed for a refund

On May 8, 2017, Edith Windsor attended the 2017 Family Equality Council's Night, an event that celebrates the accomplishments and contributions of LGBTQ+ families and communities.

from the Internal Revenue Service (IRS). The IRS denied it on the grounds that DOMA did not recognize Windsor's marriage to Spyer. Spyer and Windsor's marriage was recognized in New York. However, DOMA prevented same-sex couples from transferring money or property without subjecting them to an estate tax that opposite-sex couples whose marriages were recognized federally were not subjected to.

In 2010, Windsor filed a lawsuit against the United States. She argued that DOMA violated her constitutional right to equal protection by creating two classes of marriage: one that received rights and protections from the federal government and one that did not. In 2012, the US Second District Court of Appeals ruled in her favor, and an appeals court upheld the ruling. Finally, in 2013, the US Supreme Court found that Section 3 of DOMA was unconstitutional because it violated the Fifth Amendment. Writing the majority opinion, Justice Anthony Kennedy said the "principle purpose" of DOMA was to "impose inequality." Such a primary purpose violated a citizen's right to fair treatment. DOMA was done.

MARRIAGE EQUALITY ARRIVES AT LAST

With the federal definition of marriage struck down along with DOMA, the problem of recognition still loomed. In a case that came to be known as *Obergefell v. Hodges,* the US Supreme Court

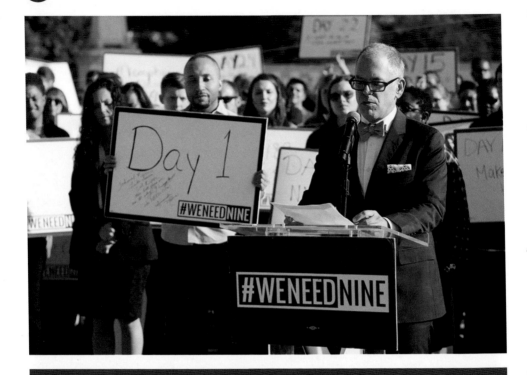

Jim Obergefell (*right*) speaks at a rally urging senators to move forward with a confirmation hearing for Merrick Garland, the man President Obama chose as the Supreme Court nominee after Justice Antonin Scalia's unexpected death in 2016.

decided on the legality and recognition of same-sex marriage on a federal level. This decision had the power to grant LGBTQ+ individuals rights they had only dreamed of. It was therefore considered the pinnacle battle in the fight for equality.

Obergefell v. Hodges was not one court case. It was six lower-court cases bundled together. The plaintiffs were sixteen same-sex couples, seven of their children, a widower, a funeral director, and an adoption agency. The cases came from Ohio

(*Obergefell v. Kasich* and *Henry v. Wymyslo*), Kentucky (*Bourke v. Beshear* and *Love v. Beshear*), Tennessee (*Tanco v. Haslam*), and Michigan (*DeBoer v. Snyder*). In each case, a plaintiff was denied a federally-mandated benefit (such as an inheritance) or privilege (such as adoption) because their spouse was the same sex. The cases were presented to the US Sixth Circuit Court of Appeals in August 2014. Soon after, the plaintiffs appealed to the US Supreme Court.

The Supreme Court justices argued vehemently against and for legalizing same-sex marriage.

KIM DAVIS

On June 26, 2015, Kim Davis gained notoriety when serving as county clerk for Rowan County, Kentucky. She defied a federal court order to issue marriage licenses to same-sex couples following the Supreme Court decision in *Obergefell v. Hodges*. Davis refused to issue licenses to same-sex couples for religious reasons. When asked under whose authority she was not issuing licenses, she replied, "Under God's authority." As a result, two same-sex and two opposite-sex couples sued Davis.

Davis argued that her decision not to issue licenses was protected under the First Amendment, specifically the clause that allows her to practice her religion as she chooses. Davis refused to issue licenses even after

(continued on the next page)

(continued from the previous page)

On September 14, 2015, Kim Davis (*center*) announces that her office will issue marriage licenses for same-sex couples in compliance with federal law.

a local judge, the US District Court of Appeals, and the Supreme Court ordered her to do so. As an elected official, she could not be fired from her position, so her law-breaking resulted in her serving time in county jail.

It wasn't until November 2015 that this saga ended. Governor Matt Bevin signed an executive order that removed the requirement of state clerks signing marriage licenses. In this way, Davis and other clerks who objected to same-sex marriage did not have to offer what they may have considered to be a seal of approval to each union. And, same-sex partners no longer faced this viable form of discrimination against their right to marry in Kentucky.

Justice Antonin Scalia was the most vocal opponent, citing in his dissent that legalizing same-sex marriage on a federal level amounted to an encroachment of state's rights. After continued debate, the court ultimately ruled in favor of the plaintiffs (5-4), finding that the Fourteenth Amendment did indeed require states to issue licenses to same-sex couples. This June 26, 2015, decision overruled the 1972 *Baker* ruling that had long been used as the foundation for refusing marriage licenses to same-sex couples.

Same-sex marriage was now the law of the land as *Obergefell* ensured that same-sex couples could finally receive benefits of marriage that had historically been denied to them. The case also overturned the same-sex marriage bans in the remaining fourteen states that had them and voided bans that prevented a state from recognizing a marriage performed outside of the state. Writing the majority opinion, Justice Kennedy stated, "No longer may this liberty be denied. No union is more profound than marriage, for it embodies the highest ideals of love, fidelity, devotion, sacrifice and family. In forming a marital union, two people become something greater than once they were." As he read the ruling, several lawyers in the courtroom wiped away tears. Outside hundreds of people waved rainbow flags and cheered, "Love has won."

CHAPTER SEVEN

MOVING BEYOND MARRIAGE

· ·

T he legalization of same-sex marriage brought to the foreground old challenges beyond marriage, ones that required increased organization and enthusiasm for the fights that had yet to be won. Basic protections such as antidiscrimination laws addressing schooling, housing, and work still varied widely across the country and threatened to collapse the momentum gained in the last decade. However, those who had been working on these issues were finally able to be joined by some of those who won marriage equality.

THE NEW BATTLEGROUND

Antidiscrimination laws emerged as one of the preeminent issues in the continuing fight for equality. As it stands today, although LGBTQ+ individuals now have the right to marry, laws don't always offer protections from being fired from a job, evicted from a home, or refused service at a

Jubilant crowds parade down Christopher Street during the 2015 New York City Gay Pride Parade. That year's parade took place two days after the Supreme Court's decision to overturn all same-sex marriage bans.

business because of sexual orientation or gender identity.

Antidiscrimination laws and protections are largely controlled on a state level. This is because EDNA, legislation that would have provided federal protection for LGBTQ+ people in the workplace, failed to gain enough support to pass on every occasion that it was introduced. However, in 2012, the Equal Employment Opportunity Commission (EEOC) affirmed that Title

VII of the Civil Rights Act of 1964 provides protection against discrimination in the workplace based on sexual orientation and sexual identity, in addition to the other explicitly listed classes of individuals it protects. The EEOC ruling only applies to federal jobs and does not extend protections to people employed in the private or public sector.

Thus far, some states have also risen to the occasion of offering LGBTQ+ people protections. States including New York and California have adopted antidiscrimination laws to bar employers from discriminating against an employee based on sexual orientation or identity, but 50 percent of the United States' LGBTQ+ population lives in states that offer them limited to no protection in the workplace, according to the Movement Advancement Project.

RELIGIOUS FREEDOM AT PLAY

In 2013, Aaron and Melissa Klein, the owners of Sweet Cakes by Melissa in Gresham, Oregon, refused to make a cake for Laurel and Rachel Bowman-Cryer's wedding. They argued that homosexuality was against their faith. Their decision to refuse service to the couple violated the Oregon Equality Act because it discriminated against a customer based on sexual orientation. Sweet Cakes by Melissa was fined $135,000.

This event is largely cited as the trigger for a vocal movement led by conservatives and right-wing politicians to call for a federal law that protects religious freedom. The crux of the issue pits two core concepts of American law against one another: the First Amendment right to freely practice religion and the right to participate free of discrimination. Many faith leaders and conservatives argued that forcing an organization or individual to conduct business in a way that does not fit with their religious beliefs infringed upon their freedom to express faith. Meanwhile civil rights activists countered that individuals were free to practice their religion so long as their actions did not discriminate against a population through the denial of equal treatment under the law. This continued disagreement became a hot election topic that represented the increasingly fractured landscape of American values and law.

REPRESENTATIONS AND ADOPTION

There remains room for improvement in popular culture and mainstream media for the portrayal and representation of LGBTQ+ identities, relationships, and families. However, many shows, books, and movies have begun to draw a more inclusive rendering of the diversity in America on big and small screens alike. Netflix's *Orange Is the New Black*, for example, showcases the story of a transgender woman played by actress and activist Laverne Cox. Amazon's *Transparent* has also been lauded by many for its deeply personal portrayal of transitioning. Still, it drew criticism for using a cisgender actor to portray the story of a transgender woman. Same-sex parents are often depicted in shows such as ABC's *Modern Family*.

Unfortunately, real-life legislation that governs and controls components of queer relationships and family decision-making lags far behind what Hollywood depicts. Adoption, for example, remains one of the thorniest issues for LGBTQ+ parents and individuals. Certain states restrict or provide conditions for adoption rooted in bias against sexual identity or orientation. States such as Alabama and Texas are considering allowing state-licensed child welfare agencies to deny LGBTQ+ people the right to adopt if it conflicts with the agency's religious beliefs. As of January 2018, no federal law existed to guarantee or combat adoption discrimination.

THE FIGHT OVER DISCRIMINATION LAWS IN RESTROOMS

When legislation passed in 2011 allowing lesbian and gay individuals to serve openly in the armed forces, it failed to include protections for transgender individuals. Two million transgender service persons were thus stuck in the shadows of DADT. On June 30, 2016, the Pentagon finally announced that transgender individuals no longer faced discharge because of their identity.

The following year presented serious setbacks, most visibly in the fight over assigned genders

Pat McCrory was the governor of North Carolina from 2013 to 2017. He signed the Public Facilities Privacy and Security Act, or HB2, into law in 2016.

and discrimination in public restrooms. House Bill 2, commonly referred to as HB2, was passed by North Carolina in March 2016. It prevented local ordinances from extending rights to the LGBTQ+ community. Its greatest controversy was that it also restricted restroom use to one's biological sex.

Critics of the bill were devastated and viewed it as one of the most discriminatory laws set into motion against LGBT individuals. They also argued that refusing to let transgender individuals use restrooms that reflected their gender identity was equally dangerous and discriminatory.

Proponents of the bill claimed that it would protect women against sexual assault and violence. They based their arguments on the assumption that sexual predators would have open access to harass or assault people in restrooms.

After passage of HB2, public outcry was monumental. Demonstrations filled the streets, and dozens of corporations and companies refused to conduct business in North Carolina. These protests and canceled contracts cost the state millions of dollars. Eventually, HB2 was replaced with HB142, a law that reset the government of North Carolina's official stance to be in line with other states that had an indifference toward the idea of protecting LGBTQ+ citizens. HB142 also mandated that cities in North Carolina weren't allowed to mandate any protections for employment discrimination or discrimination by public accommodations until 2020.

THE PULSE NIGHTCLUB SHOOTING

On June 12, 2016, the deadliest attack on the LGBTQ+ community in the history of the United States occurred. A lone gunman who had recently pledged allegiance to radical Islamist group Islamic State of Iraq and Syria entered Pulse, a gay nightclub in Orlando, Florida. He killed forty-nine people and wounded another fifty-eight. Most of the victims were Latinos.

In the aftermath of the attack, hundreds of people lined up to donate blood in an effort to help the victims. However, an FDA ban prohibited gay and bisexual men from donating blood unless they had abstained from sexual activity for at least twelve months. This regulation was an amended vestige from the AIDS era that barred many willing gay blood donors from participating.

The irony of the situation was a point many did not fail to notice. The events of that day highlighted two very important facts: violence and hate crimes continue to threaten and endanger lives, and policies continue to discriminate against the LGBTQ+ community in very real and devastating ways.

THE ELECTION THAT SHOOK THE WORLD

In 2016, an increasingly polarized nation saw the rise of nontraditional candidates pitted against career politicians in one of the most divisive elections in modern history. Members of the LGBTQ+ community and allies anxiously anticipated the verdict of whether the new presidency would turn the country away from or toward social progress.

Hillary Clinton, a career politician who served as first lady from 1993 to 2001, the senator of New York from 2001 to 2009, and the secretary of state from 2009 to 2013, emerged as the Democratic frontrunner of the election. Clinton was not an open advocate for gay marriage until 2013. However, the LGBTQ+ community seemed to have faith in her. In fact, she was endorsed by the HRC as their candidate of choice for her continued promise to advocate and work toward LGBTQ+ equality and against discrimination.

Hillary Clinton, the Democratic frontrunner of the 2016 presidential election, addresses a crowd of supporters in Louisville, Kentucky.

Donald Trump became the Republican candidate of choice by leading a campaign that promised to roll back protections for illegal immigrants and curb illegal immigration. He also promised to rein in the outsourcing of jobs, dismantle the Affordable Care Act, and increase protections for religious liberties.

Many progressives feared that a Trump presidency would dismantle much of the social and economic progress made in the last eight years. His track record on LGBTQ+ issues left much to be desired. Before his 2016 run, Trump publicly claimed that while he did not support gay marriage, he was also not especially concerned with it. However, with conservative support rallying behind him, Trump began to indicate that if elected he would consider making moves that were hostile to the queer community, including appointing justices to the Supreme Court who would be in favor of overturning *Obergefell*.

On November 8, 2016, Donald Trump won the presidential election by securing the needed votes from each state in the Electoral College.

CHALLENGES UNDER TRUMP

While President Trump had said in the past that he supported amending the Civil Rights Act of 1964 to include the category of sexual orientation and supported hate crime legislation covering sexual orientation, his presidency has been contrary to the spirit of equality. Trump selected a vice president

President Trump's time in office included some executive orders that negatively impacted the LGBTQ+ community.

whose electoral record is openly hostile to LGBTQ+ individuals, and he has signaled that he wants more constitutionalist judges in the US Supreme Court. Any nomination to the US Supreme Court could culminate in overturning *Obergefell*. President Trump has also rescinded the Fair Pay and Safe Workplaces order and withdrew a motion previously filed with the Department of Justice that sought to allow transgender students to have the right to use public school restrooms that match their gender identity.

Trump also mentioned in his campaign that he would consider passing a Religious Freedom executive order. Such an executive order would allow religious people to discriminate against LGBTQ+ people for religious reasons. The executive order that he signed in May 2017 did not allow for this type of discrimination in an absolute manner. This is not as bad as may have been expected, but it is still a step backward.

Avenues for change have often seemed invisible or unreachable, but this is not so. The past teaches that change happens when the people apply pressure to local, state, and federal levels of government. What has changed in the past few decades is that more Americans support LGBTQ+ equality than opposite it. That is a huge step forward, especially since most of the anti-LGBTQ+ legislation from the 1990s and 2000s was by popular ballot. But those who care about marriage equality must be vigilant. If the past has a lesson, it's that the fight is not over when a piece of legislation is won. Americans or politicians might be forced to vote again on marriage equality if *Obergefell* is struck down. The government might try to change how much coverage a spouse qualifies for under a new health care initiative like the American Health Care Act of 2017. Americans might have to fight again to ensure that "spouse" means a same-sex partner. Powerless as one person might feel in the face of these threats, millions have fought impossible odds and won. But the future may call on new generations to do it all again.

TIMELINE

1993 Hawaii Supreme Court decision in *Baehr v. Lewin* finds that a state statute limiting marriage to opposite-sex couples violates the state's constitution.

1994 Don't Ask, Don't Tell (DADT) is initiated. It permitted LGB individuals to serve in the armed forces as long as they didn't disclose their sexual orientation.

1996 The Defense of Marriage Act (DOMA), a response to *Baehr*, is signed into law. It was a federal law that defined marriage as a union between one man and one woman.

1997 Minnesota bans same-sex marriage with a state law that passed in the legislature.

1998 Alaska and Hawaii pass amendments banning same-sex marriage.

1999 In *Baehr v. Miike*, the Hawaii Supreme Court upholds its ban of same-sex marriage.
The Vermont Supreme Court holds that same-sex couples cannot be barred from any of the rights offered to heterosexual couples.

2000 George W. Bush is elected president.
Vermont recognizes same-sex civil unions.

2002 Nevada bans same-sex marriage.

2003 An appellate court in Massachusetts rules that same-sex marriage is legal.

2005 Kansas and Texas ban same-sex marriage.

2006 Nebraska's ban on same-sex marriage is upheld in district court.

Seven states pass marriage restrictions, including a ban in Alabama.

2007 New Jersey legalizes civil unions.

2008 Barack Obama is elected president.

2009 Iowa, Maine, and Vermont legalize same-sex marriage.

Voters in Maine overturn same-sex marriage.

2010 Obama signs legislation to repeal DADT.

New Hampshire and the District of Columbia legalize same-sex marriage.

2011 DADT officially ends.

Obama declares he will no longer defend DOMA.

New York legalizes same-sex marriage.

2012 A US Court of Appeals rules against DOMA.

2013 Same-sex marriage is legalized in California, Minnesota, Rhode Island, Delaware, New Jersey, and Hawaii.

2015 *Obergefell v. Hodges* definitively legalizes same-sex marriage nationwide.

2016 The Cherokee Nation legalizes same-sex marriage.

GLOSSARY

appeal A process of review in which a party requests a change to an official ruling.

ballot amendment An addition to a state's constitution by popular demand.

bias Unfair sentiments in favor of or against a particular point of view.

bipartisan Describing cooperation, agreement, and compromise between two major parties.

cisgender A nonnormative term for people whose gender identity matches the sex they were assigned at birth.

civil union A legally recognized union similar to marriage that holds some benefits of a marriage.

Congress The federal lawmaking body of the United States, made up of the US House of Representatives and the US Senate. Each state within the United States also has a lawmaking body that rules that state.

consensual When multiple parties agree to engage in an activity willingly and without coercion.

constitutional rights Rights defined in the US Constitution that cannot be interfered with by the government or by private entities or individuals.

Federal Marriage Amendment (FMA) A proposed amendment to the Constitution to define marriage as a union between one man and one woman.

gender identity How a person feels gender that may or may not match the assigned sex at birth.

governor The head of a state who serves as leader of the executive branch.

hate crimes Crimes that target a person or group because of their gender orientation, sexual identity, race, religion, or national origin.

heteronormative Describes a belief that heterosexuality is the only natural expression of sexuality.

homophobic Having to do with the fear of people who are attracted to people of the same sex.

lobby A professional group that seeks to change a politician or public official's position on an issue.

next of kin A legal status that allows a person to make important decisions for a person who is unable to do it on his, her, or their own behalf.

political action committee (PAC) An organization that funds candidates and political parties who advocate for the PAC's interests.

public accommodation A facility that offers services and is open to the public.

queer Originally meaning "peculiar," *queer* was later used as a derogative term for gays and lesbians and same-sex activities in the twentieth century. Queer has been reclaimed in recent decades as a term for gender minorities who are not cisgender or heterosexual.

sexual orientation A pattern of sexual or romantic attraction that is usually limited to a group of people (opposite-sex attraction, same-sex attraction). However, criteria may go beyond sexual and romantic attraction in such a way to establish orientations that hinge on attraction to intelligence, personality, and other facets of identity, and it may be that attraction is so exclusive as to only include one person instead of a whole so-called type.

transgender A term describing people whose gender identity differs from the one assigned to them at birth; not cisgender.

FOR MORE INFORMATION

The Ali Forney Center (AFC)
321 West 125th Street
New York, NY 10027
(212) 206-0574
Website: http://www.aliforneycenter.org
Facebook: @AliForney
Twitter: @AliForneyCenter
The AFC is the largest organization in the United
States dedicated to providing resources,
including housing, job preparedness, and
health care services, for LGBTQ+ youth who
are homeless.

American Civil Liberties Union (ACLU)
125 Broad Street, 18th Floor
New York, NY 10004
(212) 549-2500
Website: https://www.aclu.org
Facebook: @aclu.nationwide
Twitter: @ACLU
YouTube: @acluvideos
The ACLU works to defend the constitutional rights
of lesbian, gay, bisexual, and transgender people
through legal representation in suits against
individuals or governments.

Egale Canada Human Rights Trust
185 Carlton Street
Toronto, ON M5A 2K7

Canada
(888) 204-7777
Website: http://egale.ca
Facebook: @EgaleCanada
Twitter: @egalecanada
This organization is working toward a Canada free
of discrimination based on gender identity
and sexual orientation by promoting research,
community engagement, and education.

Lambda Legal
120 Wall Street, 19th Floor
New York, NY 10005-3919
(212) 809-8585
Website: https://www.lambdalegal.org
Facebook and YouTube: @lambdalegal
Twitter: @LambdaLegal
A nonprofit organization of litigators whose goal is
to fight for the civil rights of LGBTQ+ individuals
and those suffering from HIV.

PFLAG Canada
1554 Carling Avenue, Suite 243
Ottawa, ON K1Z 7M4
Canada
(888) 530-6777
Website: http://pflagcanada.ca
Facebook: @PFLAG
Twitter: @PFLAG
PFLAG Canada offers a variety of resources to
promote public awareness of LGBTQ+ issues,
as well as support for individuals dealing with

issues concerning sexual orientation and gender identity.

Southern Poverty Law Center (SPLC)
400 Washington Avenue
Montgomery, AL 36104
(888) 414-7752
Website: https://www.splcenter.org
Facebook: @SPLCenter
Twitter: @splcenter
Focused primarily in the Southeast, SPLC is working in the courts to help LGBTQ+ individuals achieve full equality under the law.

FOR FURTHER READING

Belge, Kathy, and Marke Bieschke. *Queer: The Ultimate LGBT Guide for Teens*. San Francisco, CA: Zest Books, 2011.

Henneberg, Susan. *LGBTQ Rights.* New York, NY: Greenhaven Publishing, 2017.

Hillstrom, Kevin. *Gay Marriage.* Farmington Hills, MI: Lucent Books, 2014.

Hollander, Barbara Gottfried. *Marriage Rights and Gay Rights*. New York, NY: Rosen Publishing, 2015.

Huegel, Kelly. *GLBTQ: The Survival Guide for Queer and Questioning Teens.* Minneapolis, MN: Free Spirit Publishing, 2003.

Kingston, Anna. *Respecting the Contributions of LGBT Americans.* New York, NY: Rosen Publishing, 2012.

Morlick, Theresa. *LGBTQ Human Rights Movement.* New York, NY: Rosen Publishing, 2017.

Pohlen, Jerome. *Gay and Lesbian History for Kids: The Century-Long Struggle for LGBT Rights.* Chicago, IL: Chicago Review Press, 2016.

Sickels, Carter. *Untangling the Knot: Queer Voices on Marriage, Relationships, and Identity*. Portland, OR: Ooligan Press, 2015.

Watson, Stephanie. *Gay Rights Movement* (Essential Library of Social Change). North Mankato, MN: ABDO Publishing, 2014.

BIBLIOGRAPHY

Alba, Alejandro. "LGBTQ Community Angered with FDA Ban on Blood Donation After Orlando Mass Shooting." *Daily News,* June 12, 2016. http://www.nydailynews.com/news/national/orlando-blood-banks-accepting-donations-mass-shooting-article-1.2670700.

Blinder, Alan, and Richard Perez-Pena. "Kentucky Clerk Denies Same-Sex Marriage Licenses, Defying Court." *New York Times*, September 1, 2015. https://www.nytimes.com/2015/09/02/us/same-sex-marriage-kentucky-kim-davis.html.

Davidson, Joe. "Obama Administration Allows Health Coverage for Same-Sex Spouse." *Washington Post*, March 26, 2012. https://www.washingtonpost.com/blogs/federal-eye/post/obama-administration-allows-health-coverage-for-same-sex-spouse/2011/04/15/gIQAddl4cS_blog.html.

Eckholm, Erik. "Next Fight for Gay Rights: Bias in Jobs and Housing." *New York Times,* June 27, 2015. https://www.nytimes.com/2015/06/28/us/gay-rights-leaders-push-for-federal-civil-rights-protections.html.

Equaldex. "LGBT Rights in United States." June 10, 2017. http://www.equaldex.com/region/united-states.

Gjelten, Tom. "In Religious Freedom Debate, 2 American Values Clash." NPR, February 28,

2017. http://www.npr.org/2017/02/28 /517092031/in-religious-freedom-debate-2 -american-values-clash.

Goodnough, Abby, and Katie Zezima. "Suit Seeks to Force Government to Extend Benefits to Same-Sex Couples." *New York Times*, March 2, 2009. http://www.nytimes.com/2009/03/03 /us/03marriage.html.

Gray, Eliza. "Edith Windsor, The Unlikely Activist." *Time*, December 11, 2011. http://poy.time .com/2013/12/11/runner-up-edith-windsor -the-unlikely-activist.

Gross, Jane. "Hiding in Uniform; Homosexuals in the Military; For Gay Soldiers and Sailors, Lives of Secrecy and Despair." *New York Times*, April 10, 1990. http://www.nytimes .com/1990/04/10/us/hiding-uniform -homosexuals-military-for-gay-soldiers -sailors-lives-secrecy.html?pagewanted=all.

GSS Data Explorer. "Homosexual Sex Relations." Accessed May 28, 2017. https:// gssdataexplorer.norc.org/variables/634/vshow.

Hevesi, Dennis. "Group Finds a 65% Rise in Bias Crime." *New York Times,* February 27, 1992. http://www.nytimes.com/1992/02/27 /nyregion/group-finds-a-65-rise-in-bias-crime .html.

Hillstrom, Kevin. *Gay Marriage.* Farmington Hills, MI: Lucent Books, 2014.

Holder, Eric. "Statement of the Attorney General on Litigation Involving the Defense of Marriage

Act." United States Department of Justice, February 23, 2011. https://www.justice.gov /opa/pr/statement-attorney-general-litigation -involving-defense-marriage-act.

Koch, Brittany Blackburn. "The Effect of *Obergefell v. Hodges* for Same-Sex Couples." *The National Law Review.* July 17, 2015. http://www .natlawreview.com/article/effect-obergefell-v -hodges-same-sex-couples.

LeBlanc, Steve. "Mass. AG Argues Against Federal Gay Marriage Ban." *Boston Globe*, May 26, 2010. http://archive.boston.com/news /nation/articles/2010/05/26/mass_ag_ argues_against_federal_gay_marriage_ban.

McKinley, James C. "Bomb Explodes at a Gay Bar, Prompting a Protest." *New York Times,* April 29, 1990. http://www.nytimes.com/1990/04/29 /nyregion/bomb-explodes-at-a-gay-bar -prompting-a-protest.html.

Obergefell et al. v. Hodges, Director, Ohio Department of Health, et al., (2015) No. 14-556. http://caselaw.findlaw.com /us-supreme-court/14-556.html.

Pew Research Center: Religion and Public Life. "Changing Attitudes on Gay Marriage." May 12, 2016. http://www.pewforum.org/2016/05/12 /changing-attitudes-on-gay-marriage.

Richardson, Bradford. "Sweet Cakes by Melissa, Christian Bakers from Oregon, Appeal $136K Fine in Gay Wedding Case." *The Washington Times,* March 6, 2017. http://www

.washingtontimes.com/news/2017/mar/6
/sweet-cakes-melissa-christian-bakers-oregon
-appeal.

Stern, Mark Joseph. "The HB2 'Repeal' Bill Is
an Unmitigated Disaster for LGBTQ Rights
and North Carolina." Slate, March 30, 2017.
http://www.slate.com/blogs/outward/2017
/03/30/hb2_repeal_bill_is_a_disaster_for
_north_carolina_and_lgbtq_rights.html.

INDEX

ABOUT THE AUTHOR

John Mazurek lives and works in Tacoma, Washington. While he is currently a high school English teacher and writer, he has worked in educational and academic publishing and maintains a keen interest in exploring topics related to social justice and history.

PHOTO CREDITS

Cover (top and bottom), pp. 68–69 Justin Sullivan/Getty Images; pp. 6–7, 65 Alex Wong/Getty Images; pp. 6–7 (background) esfera/Shutterstock.com; pp. 12–13 New York Post Archives/The New York Post/Getty Images; p. 16 Boston Globe/Getty Images; p. 19 Mark Wilson/Getty Images; pp. 21, 27, 37, 42–43, 50–51, 80 © AP Images; pp. 24–25 Cynthia Johnson/Hulton Archive/Getty Images; pp. 30–31 Carr/MCT/Newscom; pp. 34–35 Angela Jimenez/The New York Times/Redux; pp. 40–41 Gabriel Olsen/FilmMagic /Getty Images; p. 45 David Paul Morris/Getty Images; p. 48 Ray Tamarra/Getty Images; pp. 56–57 Lyn Alweis/Denver Post/Getty Images; pp. 62–63 Bloomberg/Getty Images; p. 76 Mike Pont/WireImage/Getty Images; p. 78 Zach Gibson /Getty Images; p. 83 Andrew Lichtenstein/Corbis News/Getty Images; p. 87 Chip Somodevilla/Getty Images; pp. 90–91 NurPhoto/Getty Images; p. 93 Pool/Getty Images.

Design: Michael Moy; Layout: Nicole Russo-Duca; Editor: Bernadette Davis; Photo Research: Karen Huang